SILHOUETTES

How to Make and Use Them

SILHOUETTES

How to Make and Use Them

by Jack Kramer

Drawings by Michael Valdez
Photographs by Matthew Barr

HOUGHTON MIFFLIN COMPANY   Boston   1977

**Library of Congress Cataloging
in Publication Data**
Kramer, Jack.
    Silhouettes.

    1. Silhouettes.   I. Title.
NC910.K78   741.7   76-44873
ISBN 0-395-25060-9

Printed in the United States of America

V 10 9 8 7 6 5 4 3 2 1

Contents

Introduction

Silhouette: A Likely Likeness

The word *silhouette* means the representation of something in outline. If you ever used your fingers to make the shapes of animal figures on a white wall, you were doing a form of silhouette work. Étienne de Silhouette (1709–1769), controller-general of finances under Louis XV, unintentionally gave his name to this art form. Because he tried to reduce the pensions of the French nobles, they ridiculed him by applying his name to what were considered "empty" drawings; that is, profiles. However, many such pieces came to be treasures.

Sometimes called a profile in miniature, the silhouette was as popular from 1760 to 1860 as photographs are today. Indeed, it was the only inexpensive way to have a likeness done. After 1860, a new method of picture-taking, photography, became popular, and the art of the silhouette declined. In recent years, however, silhouette work has resurfaced with vigor, probably because of its nostalgic charm. In addition, the cut black paper against a white background can capture, almost immediately, great detail and character.

While we think of silhouettes mainly as profiles of people, they lend themselves equally well to depicting animals and landscapes — almost any kind of scene you might want to preserve. The experienced silhouettist is as much an artist as a craftsman. But the making of silhouettes is a technique that can easily be learned and enjoyed by almost anyone from eight to eighty. And the variation within the world of silhouettes is tremendous. Although silhouettes in the strictest terms are cut from paper, they can also be painted. This is a versatile art that has many directions, and in this book I hope to acquaint you with the many faces of silhouettes.

SILHOUETTES

How to Make and Use Them

1

What Is a Silhouette?

Through the years silhouettes have been called shades, profiles, or shadow portraits. Basically the silhouette is an outline, usually in black — an actual depiction or representation of the shadow of a person or object. Today the most familiar form of silhouette is the hand-cut–paper type, but at one time, when silhouettes were the rage, machines were used for the cutting.

Silhouettes can also be done in color — gilded, bronzed, or silvered — to define various textures like hair and leaves. Or they can be painted on glass, board, or plaster. But it is the *outline* that is important — the sharp division between the edge of the profile or object and the background.

Paper Silhouettes

The typical silhouette is cut from black paper and mounted on a white or pastel-colored board. The paper is cut away from the *outside* of the silhouette; the central part is mounted onto the board. The silhouette is then framed with glass or hung on the wall unframed. This type of silhouette is called a solid cut. You can first outline the silhouette and then cut it out or — with some practice — you can cut out the silhouette freehand by looking at an object as you cut.

Another style of silhouette cutting is the hollow cut. Here the negative area is used as the silhouette; it is the white mounting board showing through the paper that is the silhouette. (Detail work, such as buttonholes, collar, or lapels, is also done in hollow-cut style.) A rare type of silhouette is cut from white paper and then mounted on a *black* background.

In typical silhouettes — the solid cuts or hollow cuts on white board — the silhouette is put on a board with paste and the board is framed like a painting.

Painted Silhouettes

Painted silhouettes on illustration board require more skill, equipment, and time than paper silhouettes. Any pattern in this book can be traced on rigid board and then filled in with black paint, but for pure simplicity, I choose the paper-type silhouette.

A typical paper silhouette mounted on a white board shows distinctly the features of the small boy. This silhouette was done by a professional silhouettist at an amusement park.

Although silhouettes are usually associated with profiles, nature scenes can be used too. This bird made a handsome subject for silhouette work.

Both the solid-cut and hollow-cut type of silhouette are shown here. The leaf on the left is a hollow cut mounted on a white board; the leaf on the right, a solid cut mounted on white board.

A paper silhouette using hollow-cut work for definition.

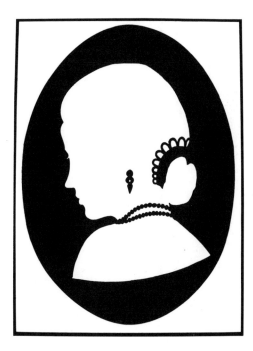

This example of a rare type of silhouette shows the profile cut from white paper and mounted on black board.

A silhouette can also be painted on the reverse side of a piece of glass for a different and quite pleasing effect. If done properly, the silhouette seems to float in space. Mark the outline in grease pencil on the glass and fill in the object; you must do this with great precision and with even strokes, because any ragged edges will ruin the silhouette. (See Chapter 5.)

If you paint your silhouette on convex glass and then place the glass an inch from the mounting board, you will get still another effect — a handsome shadow picture. (See Chapter 11.)

This style of silhouette was popular years ago and, to the delight of many, seems to be making a comeback.

Helpful Hints

1. Remember that the most important part of any silhouette is its outline.
2. Silhouettes must be sharp; never ragged.
3. If you are doing profiles, omit details like eyes, ears, and hair, because paper silhouetting is a two-dimensional art.
4. If details are to be inserted in silhouettes, they should be done by hollow-cut work.
5. Silhouettes look best when mounted alone on a plain background.
6. A silhouette should never be too large. If the silhouette is to be a framed picture, make it a miniature, with the head (if this is a portrait) never more than 4 inches in height.
7. Scale and proportion are paramount if you are doing scenes, flowers, leaves, and so forth.
8. Do not mix cut and painted work on the same surface.
9. If you want to add color, do so very carefully; just add touches to hair or apparel. (See Chapter 12.)

This seashell was better suited to a painted silhouette than a paper one because of its intricate outline.

2

What You Will Need

Silhouettes are inexpensive to make, take relatively little time to trace and cut, and require simple materials and tools. With these, and aided by a trained eye and some experience, you will soon be framing your creations and delighting your friends with visually exciting silhouettes!

Scissors

You will need two good pairs of scissors. Forget fifty-cent scissors; you need fine embroidery scissors. One pair should be blunt-tipped; the other, sharp-tipped. One pair should have blades 1 to 1-1/2 inches long; the other pair should be somewhat longer. Make sure the finger holes feel comfortable when you hold the scissors, and check that the scissors cut all the way along the blade from the rivet to the point (many scissors make only half-cuts). The cut must be firm and long so that you get the continuous outline you need for silhouettes. You should oil the joints of the scissors occasionally with sewing machine oil; but be sure that none of the oil gets on the blades, or you will ruin your silhouette surface. And use your scissors *only* for cutting paper, or you will dull the blades.

From time to time you will have to sharpen your scissors; buy a carborundum whetstone from a hardware store or a glass supplier. This stone is usually rectangular, about 3 inches long. Sharpen your scissors by holding each blade at an angle and stroking each blade firmly and evenly against the stone. You must preserve the concave shape of the blades. If you do not, you will tear your silhouettes when you cut them.

Razor-Knife

You can sometimes use a single-edged razor blade to do hollow-cut detail work, but more often a razor-knife is needed. This is a wooden or metal handle with a blade inserted at an angle in the tip. The most commonly used razor-knife is the X-Acto, which comes in many sizes. I use a Number One X-Acto knife for my detail-cutting and it is very satisfactory.

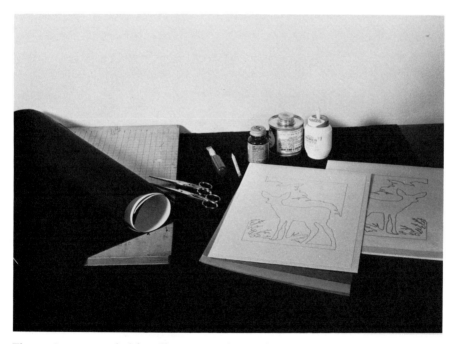

The equipment needed for silhouette work costs little: a board, two pairs of scissors, a cutting knife, adhesives, carbon paper, and mounting board.

Papers

Silhouette paper is the best for cutting silhouettes, but almost any kind of opaque paper will do, including brown kraft paper. The surface finish of the paper you use will greatly influence the character of the silhouette, and it is essential that it be easy to cut. Tissue or crepe paper will not work for silhouettes; they are too flimsy.

Silhouette Paper

Silhouette paper has a handsome dull black finish; the underside is white. This paper, easy to cut, comes in inexpensive 24-by-30-inch sheets. Silhouette paper shows creases or folds readily, so handle it with care.

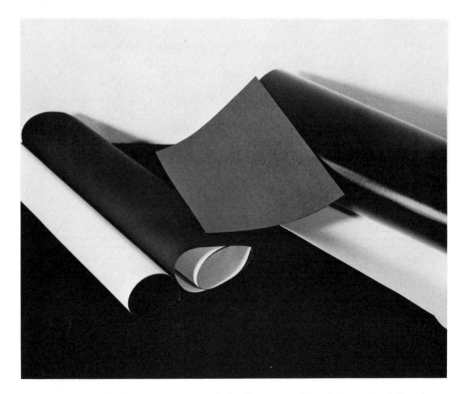

Various types of silhouette paper include the true type at left, construction paper in center, and, at right, Chrome Craft or Glow black heavy paper.

Black construction paper, sometimes called silhouette paper although it really is not, is available in packages of 50 sheets. Most construction paper is black on both sides and has a somewhat textured surface.

Medium-Weight Papers

There are a vast number of opaque papers in this category, all of which are fine for cutting. Medium-weight papers, thicker than tissue or crepe paper, include blotting paper, colored construction paper, wallpaper, wrapping paper, and shelf paper. These are easy to work with and will not crumple or crease under pressure. They cut easily, and any paste readily sticks to them.

The true silhouette is black, but sometimes opaque dark-colored construction papers — blue or purple, red or orange, brown or green, or whatever — may be used. Colored-paper silhouettes can be quite handsome. For instance, if you want to make a striking Christmas card, a dark green tree or a red Santa, mounted on white or pastel-colored stock, is dramatic. For Easter, a dark violet bunny mounted against yellow paper would also be effective.

Quite frankly, I think silhouettes should be black, but for those festive occasions when you want a distinctive handmade piece, colored papers can certainly be used.

Heavier Papers

Any heavy drawing paper, poster paper, wrapping paper, or photo album paper can also be used for silhouettes, as long as it is opaque. These are tough papers, so somewhat more pressure is needed to cut them, but they do cut cleanly. Heavier papers, not as flimsy as medium-weight papers, need a somewhat stronger adhesive. All these papers are relatively inexpensive.

Matte and Shiny Papers

Pastel and blotting papers, poster boards, and miscellaneous opaque colored illustration boards are also suitable for silhouettes but are harder to cut because they are heavy. However, the different type of surface will lend a different character to a silhouette. For example, Chrome Craft (or Chrome Glow) paper, which has a shiny black side and a white underside, can be exquisite.

You can buy paper for your silhouettes at art stores, printing offices, home decorator stores, stationers, photography stores, and craft shops. Kraft paper (excellent for practicing), which makes a good silhouette, is free if you use grocery bags, and wrapping paper has possibilities too.

Each type of paper has its own characteristics. Once you start handling a specific kind of paper, you can determine just how suitable it is for the project you have in mind.

Adhesives

Adhesives are important because, if they are not of the proper quality, they can ruin a silhouette. Here is a rundown on adhesives:

Paste

Paste dries without discoloring the silhouette or the mount, and a little goes a long way. Generally called paper paste, it comes in small unbreakable bottles that have an insert brush. You will use paste to stick layers of paper together when cutting more than one specimen at a time and also to mount your silhouettes.

Rubber Cement

Specifically made for sticking paper to paper, rubber cement is fast-drying and nonwrinkling and comes in a glass jar with its own brush applicator. You can easily remove excess cement by rubbing it with a white rubber-cement eraser. Rubber cement's one disadvantage is that if it is left too long in the bottle, it gets very thick and then requires the addition of a thinner. However, a strong plus in rubber cement's favor is that if you want to remove your silhouette after the cement has set, you can just drench the silhouette paper with thinner and quickly remove the silhouette with tweezers. (Keep pouring on thinner if it starts to dry.) The thinner evaporates, leaving no stain.

Rubber cement is also available in tubes. I have not been able to determine the difference between the products that come in tubes and the less expensive rubber cement sold in jars.

Paper Cement

This is a highly satisfactory adhesive quite similar to rubber cement (and sometimes even called rubber cement!). There is no curling, shrinking, or wrinkling of the paper when you use paper cement, and you can remove excess or misplaced cement by rubbing it with your finger. Note that paper cement does congeal in cold weather. Paper cement comes in cans with a brush applicator.

Elmer's Glue-All

Elmer's Glue-All comes in a plastic container that is difficult to open. It is an excellent adhesive for most uses, but is not as good for paper work as the other adhesives mentioned in this chapter.

Adhesive Sprays

Available under many trade names, adhesive sprays may do more harm than good; aerosols are under government scrutiny because of possible damage to the ozone layer in the atmosphere. Also, aerosols are very expensive, so I do not recommend them.

Except for paper paste, all adhesives are highly flammable, and some have toxic fumes, so use adhesives only in well-ventilated places. Avoid letting adhesives remain on your skin for a long period or you may develop a rash. Always read bottle or container labels and carefully follow directions. Finally, keep all glues and adhesives on high shelves, out of the reach of children.

Brushes

Most paper or rubber cements and pastes come with suitable brush applicators. But it is wise to have on hand smaller and larger brushes.

If you do a lot of silhouette work, buy some pointed and tapered brushes for applying glues; they will simplify gluing at the edges of the paper. You want brushes made of hair; these are soft and suitable for small work. Bristle brushes are too stiff. Take care of all brushes, and clean and wipe them carefully after each use.

Other Materials

You will also need pencils, masking tape or drawing pins, erasers, and a flat surface, like a desk or board, to work on. And don't forget tracing pencils and art gum erasers.

3

Cutting and Mounting Silhouettes

Cutting a silhouette takes a certain amount of patience and concentration; it is a wonderful way to keep your mind working and your fingers busy. To get the "feel" of the scissors and paper, first have a few practice sessions; just cut random shapes and forms.

When you are ready to make your silhouette, lay a piece of silhouette paper, with the *white* side facing you, on a drawing board or table. Secure the paper at each corner with masking tape or drawing pins. Draw the outline of your subject on the sheet. (If you are using a pattern from this book, put carbon paper between it and the silhouette paper and secure it with pins or tape.) After you have made the pattern, remove the paper from the drawing board. Feed the paper into the scissors in a counterclockwise direction if you are right-handed; in the opposite direction if you are left-handed. In other words, *pull* the paper toward you as you cut; never push it away from you.

Keep the scissor blades upright and try to maintain them in this position rather than letting the blades lean to the left or right. Do as

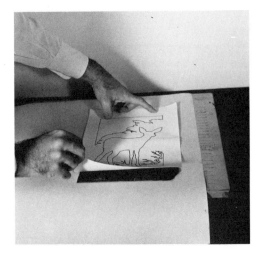

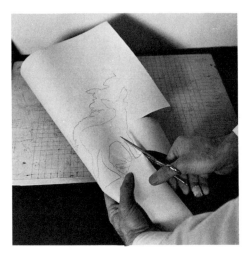
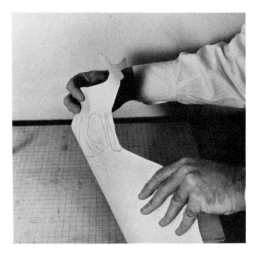

much cutting as possible from below so that the position of the scissors will help support the work and also enable you to see more clearly what you are cutting.

For hollow-cut work when you have intricate patterns — scalloped leaves, buttonholes, or such — feed the paper into the scissors in a clockwise direction. In this kind of work you do more snipping than stroke-cutting (using the whole blade). Always cut complicated parts first. Many times hollow-cut detail work will defy the scissors and you will find it better to use the razor-knife. In this case, the pattern is left on the board and the parts to be removed are cut away with the razor-knife.

Mounting

The cut silhouette comes alive when you mount it on a flat surface. Mounting both preserves and displays a silhouette. You can cement a silhouette to one of the stiff boards described below and then frame the board and use it as a picture. Or you can mount the silhouette on glass — a somewhat different but still simple process.

OPPOSITE PAGE

Above left:
Silhouette paper showing white side and black surface. Workboard.

Above right:
Pattern designed from this book is placed on carbon paper on white side of silhouette paper. Be sure to use the heavy-line pattern.

Middle left:
Masking tape or pins are used to hold pattern in place while tracing is done; be sure the silhouette paper doesn't slip.

Middle right:
Pattern and carbon paper removed; tracing is on white surface of silhouette paper.

Below left:
Cutting of pattern is started.

Below right:
Partial cutting of pattern.

Turn over the pattern so that it faces in the right direction.

The complete picture — the light-line pattern — is now traced on rigid board.

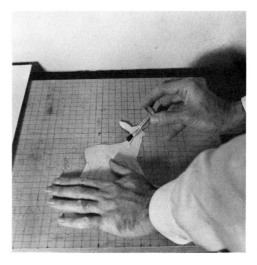

Cement is applied to back of cut pieces.

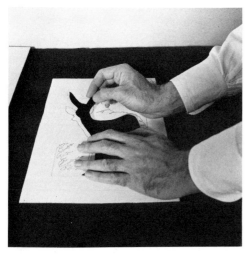

Pieces are pasted to board.

The completed silhouette, mounted on board, and ready for framing.

To mount a silhouette without adhesives, enclose it in a plastic envelope.

Cut out the plastic envelope to shape of frame you are using and set directly on glass. Cover with solid piece of cardboard (at left).

Mounting Without Adhesives

If you would rather not glue paper silhouettes on boards, there is another way, more elaborate but also effective, to get the silhouette ready for framing. In this process no adhesive is used; an envelope made from a plastic (acetate) sheet holds the silhouette. You can buy acetate sheets at art stores or stationery stores.

To follow this method, lay the plastic sheet on a flat surface. Place the silhouette where you want it, leaving proper margins at top, bottom, and sides. Now fold over the plastic and secure it by making an envelope fold that interlocks at the top. The static electricity of the plastic will hold the silhouette in place when you frame the silhouette. The "sandwich" of silhouette and plastic is then covered with an appropriate mat. Board is used to back the silhouette and the usual process of framing can be done.

Mounting Boards

The background board for your silhouette is important because it serves as the mounting board as well. In other words, it is used for more than just a backing or support; the board highlights your silhouette. Mounting boards should be suitably stiff or they will disintegrate in time. Crescent board or display board is generally used and can be purchased in cut sizes at art shops. Most silhouettes

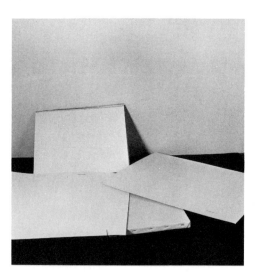

Various types of mounting boards for silhouettes.

are mounted on white or off-white boards, but often a pastel-colored board, such as matte gray or beige, is appropriate too. However, white is the color you will usually be working with, because silhouettes look best against a stark white background.

Besides crescent or display board, there are six other types of board to consider.

Bristol board: Somewhat thin but quite rigid; a handsome white.

Millboard: Very tough and rigid, but generally available only in gray.

Strawboard: This straw-colored ridged cardboard comes in various thicknesses. Not as appropriate for silhouettes as Bristol board, but it is free if you use discarded shipping boxes.

Chipboard: This brown board is made of compressed wood chips and is not too suitable for silhouettes.

Pasteboard: Pasteboard is a good smooth strong board available in white and quite good for silhouette work.

Poster board: Rigid and very durable; comes in white and has shiny finish.

Once you decide what kind of board you want, have it cut. It should usually be 2 inches larger on each side than the silhouette. To mount a silhouette on a board, first decide exactly where the silhouette is to be placed. Most often, you will want the silhouette in the center of the board, so with a pencil mark off margins on each end and the top and bottom with a center point. Then on the back of the silhouette (the white side), mark its center point (measure across the head if it is a profile).

Gluing

When you are ready to glue your silhouette, put it down, white side up, on clean newspaper or scrap paper; be sure to apply paste or glue only to the area you want to be adhered. If you are sloppy, surrounding areas of the paper will stick to the silhouette or leave a slight residue on the surface of the silhouette edge that could cause stain on the finished piece.

Work outward across the edges when gluing to avoid dragging glue underneath and getting it on the face side of the silhouette. Paper usually stretches when it has glue on it, so wait a few moments before turning it over and putting it in place on the board. Always lift the silhouette carefully, lay it in place gently, and press it lightly from the center, smoothly working any air bubbles or excess glue to the edge, where you can rub it off (if it is rubber or paper cement). Keep the paper as flat as possible while it is drying. (Sometimes I put a heavy book on top of the paper.)

Mounting on Glass or Acrylic

A silhouette can be mounted directly onto glass or acrylic. Clean the glass with alcohol, to dissolve grease and remove dust and dirt. Apply a thin coat of paper cement to the back of the silhouette (white side), spreading it with your fingers. Get a thin even coat. Make sure the silhouette is firmly in place by pressing it with your fingers and a damp sponge to make sure all parts are completely adhered. Turn the glass over — if you see any air bubbles under the silhouette, work them out carefully with your fingers.

With a sponge and water, or with your fingers, clean away excess paper cement from the glass. This must be done carefully so as not to disturb the delicate parts of the cutting. If stubborn glue spots remain, put some vinegar and water on a cotton swab and gently rub out the spot. Back the silhouette with white board or other suitable backing material. Frame with glass or plastic overlay.

4

Practice Session

When you finish your first silhouette, you may think you have
performed magic. You will have a total likeness of your subject,
whether it is a profile of a person, a flower, or an animal. But the craft
of silhouette-making has nothing to do with magic. It is a matter of
working carefully with your mind, your eyes, and your hands to
master the craft. But if first attempts are not successful, do not give
up; practice, as we have often been told, makes perfect.

Because we want to get you started quickly, we include in this part
of the book three sample silhouettes for you to duplicate. These
samples are for practice, but I'll bet you won't discard them — they
will be suitable for framing if you follow the instructions.

First let us look at the supplies you will need for the practice
session:

Materials Needed

One sheet of *pencil* carbon paper
One sheet of silhouette paper
One piece of cardboard

Two pairs of scissors (one pair, blunt-tipped; the other pair, sharp-tipped)
Glue
Level table or board
Masking tape or pins
Pencils
Erasers
Razor-knife

Practice Session

We include three patterns for your practice:
1. Rose
2. Bird
3. Sailboat

Each pattern is divided into sections, which cover two pages for each picture. The third page contains the pattern for the completed silhouette. A photo of the finished silhouette is also included to guide you.

You are now ready to begin:

1. Slip a piece of pencil carbon paper under the first section of the pattern and on top of the silhouette paper (white side up). Be sure the carbon side is against the silhouette paper. Secure all three papers with masking tape or drawing pins at each corner.

2. With a pencil, outline the pattern onto the silhouette paper through the carbon paper. *Remember:* Do this for both pages, so that you have all pieces of the complete silhouette. Don't forget to trace all of the pieces.

3. Cut out the pieces of silhouette paper with a scissors. The patterns are drawn in reverse, so when you turn them over they will be facing in the right direction.

4. Using carbon paper, trace the complete pattern from the third page directly on the mounting board. Place the cut pieces where they belong and then glue them in place. Use the photo to guide you.

5. When you have completed the silhouette, the rose, the bird, or the sailboat is ready for framing.

You can do one silhouette, or you can use all three patterns to help you get the touch. Then move on to making your own silhouettes.

Completed rose

Completed bird

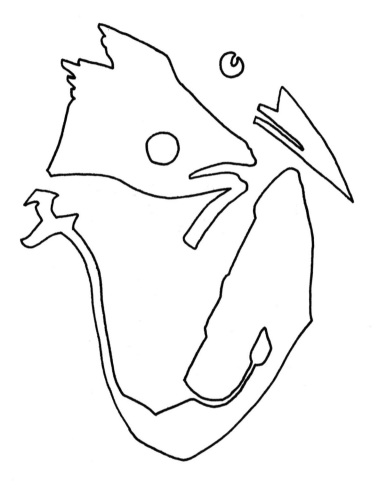

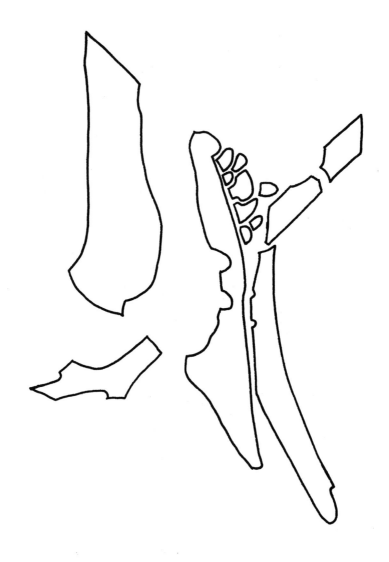

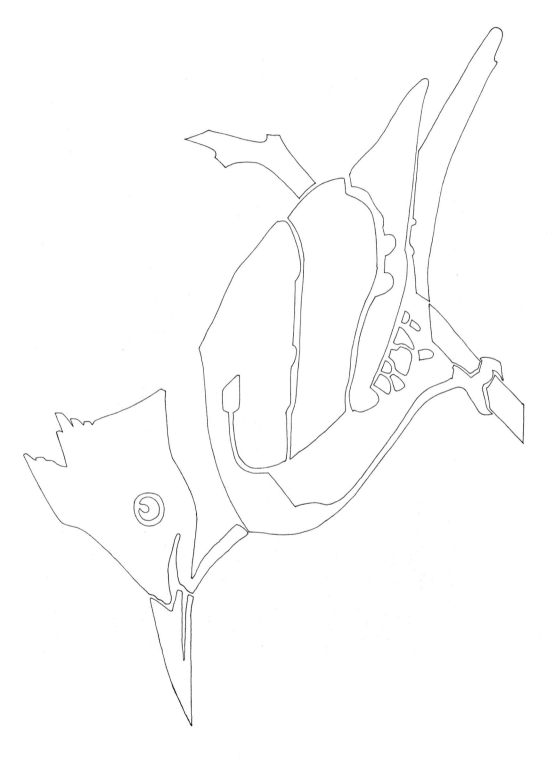

Completed sailboat

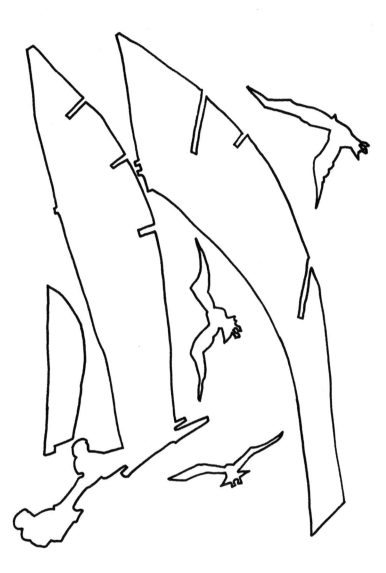

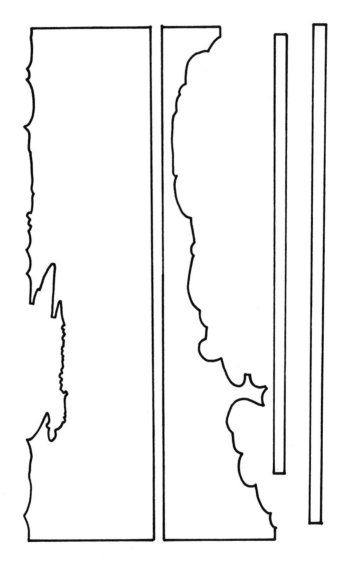

Your Own Silhouettes

It's a lot of fun to do silhouettes of members of your family; children especially get a kick out of having their silhouettes done. Making one is easy and inexpensive, and a person's profile, like his signature, is authentic, unique. You can also do a flower arrangement, your cat (if it will sit still a few minutes), or whatever strikes your fancy. But the profile is probably the easiest.

Materials Needed

Sketching paper — one sheet
Grid paper (1/4-inch grid) — one sheet
One sheet of cardboard
One sheet of silhouette paper
One sheet of pencil carbon paper
Glue or rubber cement
Scissors
Pencils
Erasers
Level table
Razor-knife

Helpful Hints for Profile Silhouettes

You can, of course, proceed directly to sketching the profile of a person or object without reading this section. However, if you have not done any art work before, I suggest you do read what follows, because it will help you capture the essence of silhouette-sketching.

The human profile can be divided into separate parts; indeed, if you look at a person in profile, your eyes will naturally scan the brow, nose, upper lip, chin, neck, and the shape of the head. As your eyes scan the profile, your hand should draw it accordingly in just about the same sequence:

1. The arch of the front of the head to where the hair starts
2. The contour of the forehead to the eyebrow
3. The space between the eyebrow and the start of the nose

4. The nose line to where the lip starts
5. The upper lip
6. The space between the upper lip and bottom lip
7. The space between the bottom lip and the start of the chin line
8. The shape of the chin and the under part of the chin
9. The neck
10. The shape of the head and the hairline

Each of these is a part of the profile; together, they make up the whole. As you notice the parts of the profile, you will also notice that there is always a salient feature. Or there may be more than one. Perhaps, for example, there is a slight hump in the nose. Maybe the chin line recedes, or the lip is especially thin or broad. It is these features you must be certain to include in your silhouette.

How to Do "Shadow" Profiles

Tack a sheet of white paper (12 by 16 would be the minimum size on which to get a silhouette image) on a blank wall somewhere in your home. The subject should be 2 to 3 feet from the paper and should assume a profile pose, in a position to cast the shadow on the center of the paper. Be sure the subject is comfortable because the pose must be held for 3 to 5 minutes; any movement will ruin the silhouette. Place an ordinary reading lamp at the correct angle to throw the shadow on the wall. You are now ready to draw the likeness. Use a soft lead

To do your own profile silhouettes, tack up large sheet of white paper on wall.

Have subject stand about 2 to 3 feet from wall, with profile cast on white paper. (Use a lamp to define shadow.) Sketch profile from side as subject poses.

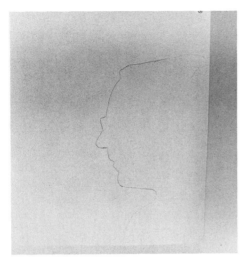

The finished outline of profile

Use grid paper to reduce the large profile.

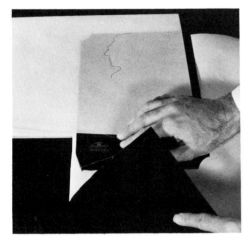

Put grid paper pattern over carbon paper over silhouette paper and draw the profile.

Cut out profile and apply adhesive.

Paste profile on white board.

pencil and carefully outline the silhouette; stay to one side of the paper so that your shadow will not disturb the silhouette. Draw quickly and deftly; no nervous or wavering lines. (Now you see why we had the practice session!)

When the drawing is finished, remove it from the wall. You now want to reduce the drawing because silhouettes look best in small scale; rarely do they succeed in large sizes. To reduce the silhouette, take a sheet of grid or graph paper and, using the boxes as guides, make pencil dots on the lines, following the outline of the original drawing. When all the dots are in, connect the lines — you will have reproduced the larger silhouette but in a smaller size.

Place the carbon paper under this reduced drawing and on top of the silhouette paper (white side up) and trace the lines. Cut off the excess margins of the silhouette paper and then carefully cut out the profile. Glue and mount the silhouette on a backing board. The silhouette is now ready for framing, or it can be placed on a wall as it is.

Follow the same procedure for still lifes, like a bowl of fruit or a floral arrangement, or for a pet.

Frame silhouette.

5

Silhouettes Painted
on Glass

Paper silhouettes shared the limelight with painted silhouettes in the mid-1800s. Some profilists swore that paper was the only true silhouette, but people who painted likenesses insisted that painting was the only true approach.

There were two basic ways of achieving the painted silhouette. The likeness was painted on a white or neutral-colored board or other suitable rigid material, or more often was painted on clear glass (which we talk about here). The painted silhouette gave the profilist more scope: the artist could embellish the background in various ways; he could use painted motifs as borders; he could add slight burnishing with gold and silver. If the silhouette was on glass, the artist would use finely etched lines or Chinese white to provide detail and dimension; often he would etch the silhouette handsomely in gold.

The silhouette painted on glass involves somewhat more skill; it is not unlike the art of painting in watercolor or oils.

I must admit that I prefer paper silhouettes but the glass silhouette is certainly charming too.

Painting On Glass

Because of the brilliant effect and distinctive quality of the silhouette on glass, I recommend highly this method of painting the silhouette, even for the beginner; it is quite exciting and satisfying. All you need are paints, a grease pencil, and a flat sheet of glass, in addition to the materials described in Chapter 2. After a few experiments you will find it easy to do the silhouette on glass.

Glass

Glass comes in several thicknesses; for silhouettes you want standard window glass of 1/16- or 1/8-inch thickness. The first thickness is designated SSB; the latter, DSB. Glass comes in standard sizes: 12 by 16 inches, 16 by 20 inches, and so forth. The standard size is based on 2-inch increments. If, for a particular purpose, you want a pane of glass 14-1/4 by 14-1/2 inches, you must pay for a piece 16 by 16 and have it cut, so it is best to stay with stock sizes and get your money's worth.

Process

For painting silhouettes, first draw the outline on the glass with colored grease pencil and then apply black paint to the figure or object. If you use a pattern from this book, trace it on white paper, cut out the paper, and then tape the paper pattern to the glass and with a grease pencil mark the outline on the glass. (You may move the pieces of tape one at a time if you want to draw the complete outline. But this will probably not be necessary if you use only a few narrow strips.) You may also place the pattern on a flat surface such as a desk or table and put a sheet of glass over it. Then trace the pattern with a grease pencil. There is little difference in the process and either method may be used. Remove tape and pattern and paint the silhouette. When it is dry, turn over the glass. (The silhouette is on the reverse side, shining through.) Back with a white or pastel board and frame.

If you have your own pattern, follow these steps:

1. Clean and polish the glass so that it is free of lint and dust.
2. Make a paper pattern and cut it out.
3. Place the pattern on a desk or table; lay a sheet of glass over it. Trace pattern with a grease pencil. (Or you can draw your own pattern on the glass freehand with a grease pencil.)
4. Using the proper paints, paint in the silhouette.

Paints and Application

Art stores carry a variety of paints that can be applied to glass; flat black or other dark colors will work fine. These are sometimes called poster colors, other times, tempera. (Do *not* use a translucent glass paint.)

Applying the paint to the glass surface requires a steady hand and some experience. You should have some ability with brush and stroke. First attempts are likely to be not wholly satisfactory, but after a few tries you can master this unusual form of silhouette. Use a steady hand and a simple pattern at first (such as the ones shown in this book). Do not thin the paint; a very thin paint is difficult to apply and may not cover surfaces evenly. Remember that you want a solid opaque surface for silhouettes.

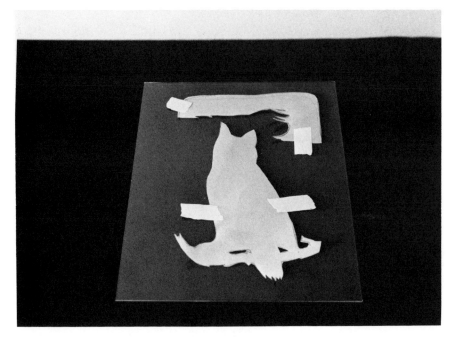

Trace the pattern onto sketch paper. Cut out pieces and tape to glass.

Painting the Silhouette

Take your best brush and put a little black paint on it. Now carefully trace over the line of the red grease pencil outline pattern that is on the reverse side of the glass. Keep your hand steady but not tense; if you tremble, the outline will be jagged. To steady your hand, rest it on a matchbox or a tiny block of wood. Doing your painting on a horizontal rather than a vertical plane (it is better to have the work under your hand than facing it) gives you greater control.

When the painted outline is dry, erase your grease pencil outline from the other side of the glass. Now start filling in the outline. This requires more care than you may think; you do not want to overrun the outline or get an uneven surface. Now you can use one of two ways to fill in the outline. Either paint it and let the paint dry, and then repeat the process twice or you might prefer to use the more professional way by hatching. (This takes more time than flat painting, but gives an even surface.) To hatch, paint a series of horizontal lines across your silhouette and then repeat the process with vertical lines. Keep the lines straight and fine and paint them as close to one another as you can. Try not to overlap strokes. Overlapping strokes results in a patchy silhouette. Always start at the top of the silhouette and work downward so that you do not touch your finished surface and so that you can judge the progress of the work.

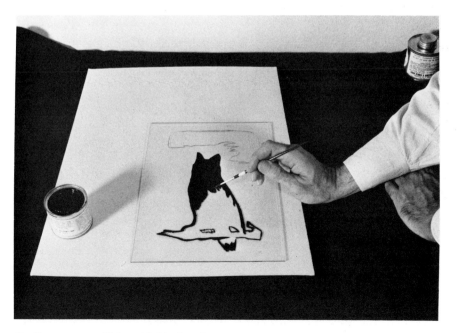

Outline pattern; fill in with black paint.

Painting of owl partly done

Completed paint-on-glass silhouette (glass has been turned over)

Backings

The painted silhouette on glass is usually backed with white or neutral-colored board. However, there is nothing wrong, and, in fact, everything all right, in using metallic papers and aluminum foil as background. Any change of paper will create a totally different effect in the silhouette art. It is a matter of choice, so by all means experiment — it's half the fun!

Three-Dimensional Effects

I notice that there is a renaissance of the painted silhouette. Generally the ones I see in stores are of nature scenes. The silhouette has been painted on one piece of glass, and then a background of a photograph or other painting has been placed behind the glass silhouette (there is a 1/2-inch air space between the glass and background). Both surfaces, the background photograph or montage and the glass, are framed together. This type of silhouette work creates a three-dimensional effect and is quite handsome.

For a slightly different effect, apply one silhouette directly to the glass and apply another silhouette to a white board in a different position. Then affix the glass pane to white board and put another glass pane on top of this. Now frame the two glass panes and the board. This works well for nature scenes, but the double glass isn't necessary for profiles.

6

Gallery of Silhouettes

In this chapter you will find a variety of patterns for silhouettes you can make. I have included flowers and animals, sailboats and landscapes, as well as such objects as locomotives and automobiles — something, I hope, for almost every taste.

Using Book Patterns

There are two patterns for each silhouette. Follow these steps to make your silhouettes:

1. Use a level working surface, such as a desk or table or drawing board.
2. Trace the heavy-lined pattern (using carbon paper) onto the white surface of silhouette paper.
3. Cut out the silhouette. Use scissors for long lines and curves; a razor-knife for intricate details.
4. Using carbon paper again, trace the light-lined pattern on a board or rigid background to guide you in the cementing process.
5. Apply cement to the white surface of the cut-out pieces and apply them to the traced pattern on the board.
6. Mat and frame the silhouette.

To help guide you further in applying the silhouette, I have included a small photograph of the finished silhouette as it was done in my workshop here.

The heavy-lined patterns are drawn in reverse; when you turn them over, the black surface will face in the proper direction to correspond to the light-lined patterns. The extra thickness of the heavy-lined patterns is to take into account the breadth of the cutting and the line itself.

Making Other Silhouettes

Once you have done a few silhouettes, using the patterns in this book, you might want to make your own silhouettes from magazine pictures. Or you might want to do freehand sketches from nature or of another kind of object and make silhouettes from them. The process is the same as that outlined above except that you will be using your own patterns, and the patterns can be made in the manner described above.

Flower pattern #1 — Dogtooth violet

Flower pattern #2 — Wildflower

Flower pattern #3 — Mariposa lily

Zebra

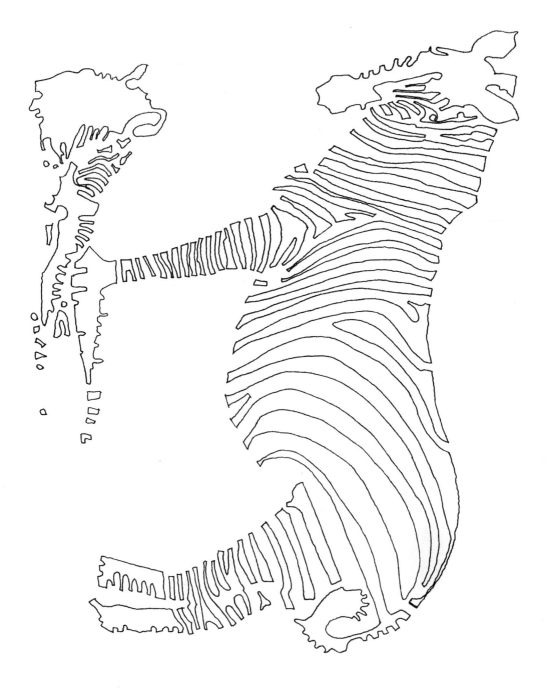

Rabbit

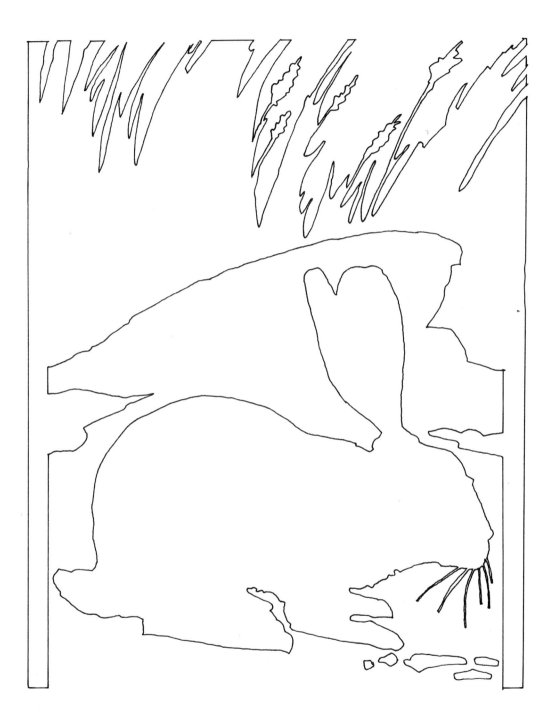

Cranes

Deer

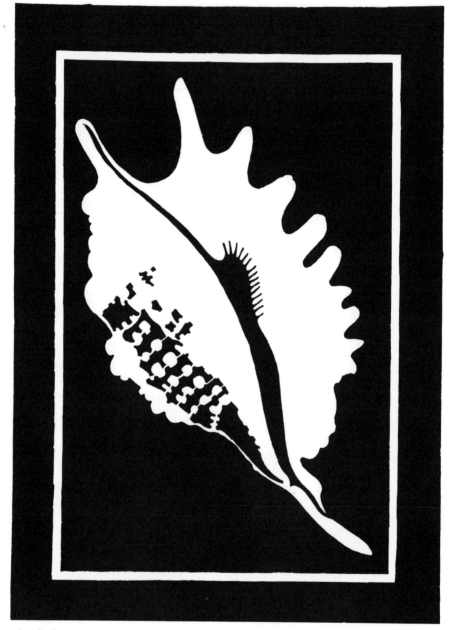

Seashell

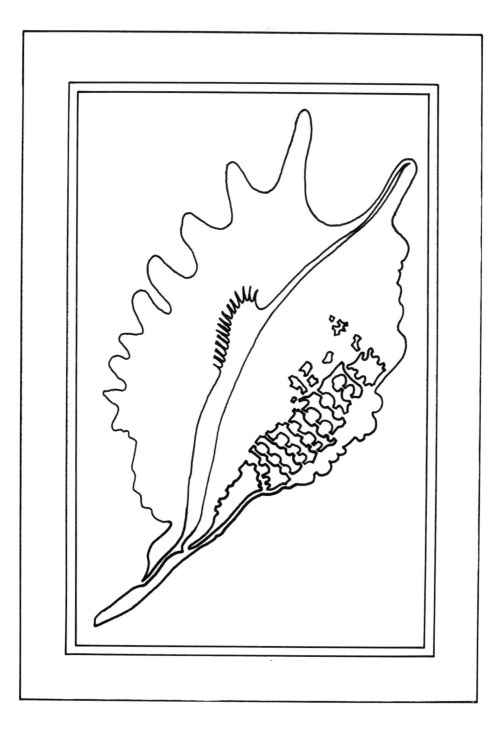

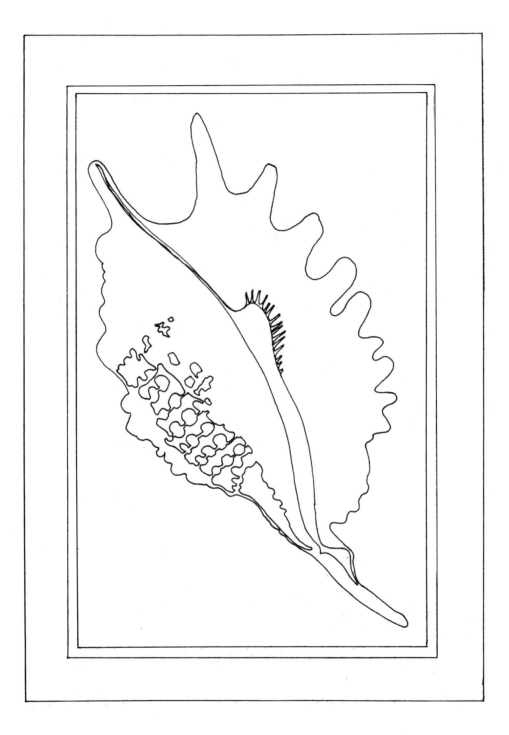

Porpoises

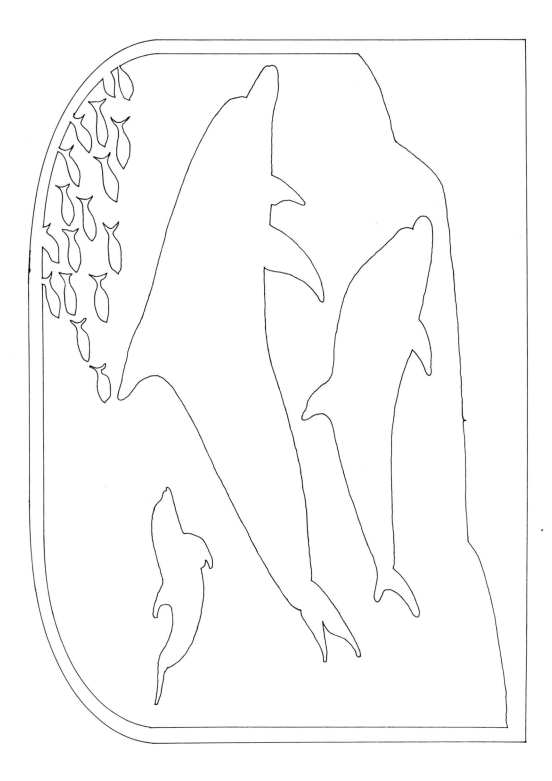

Tropical fish

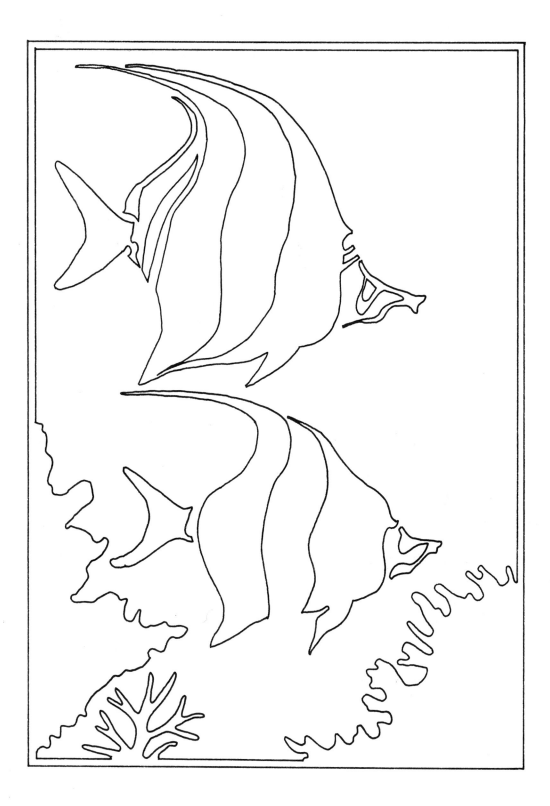

Japanese landscape

Country meadow

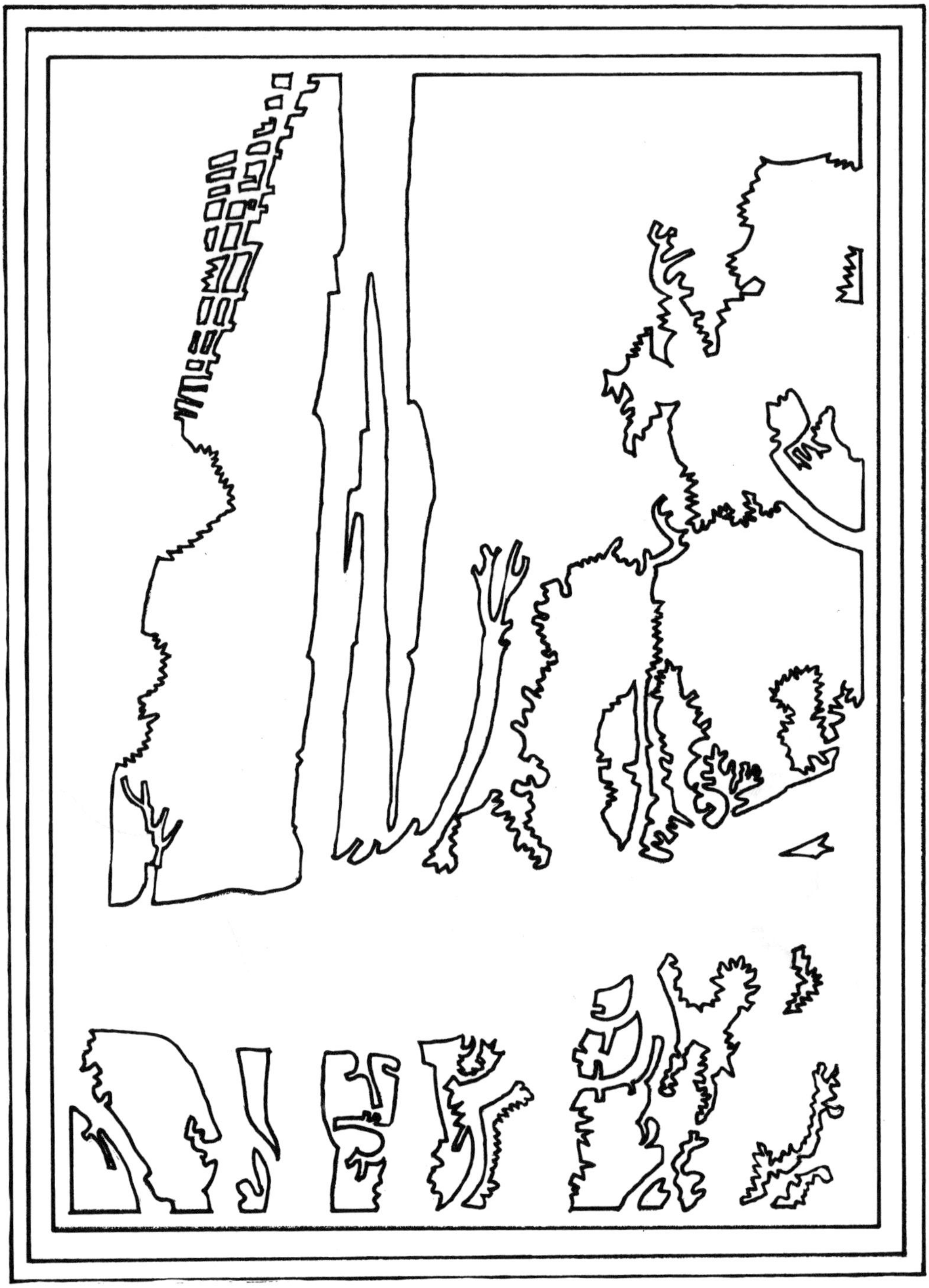

Windmill

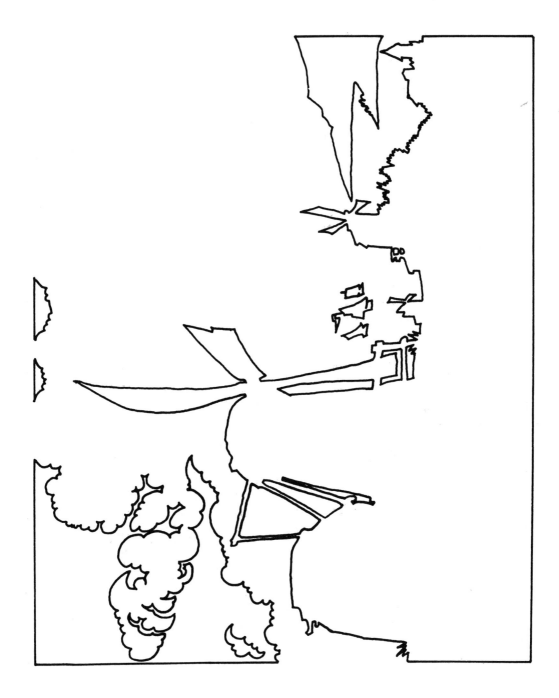

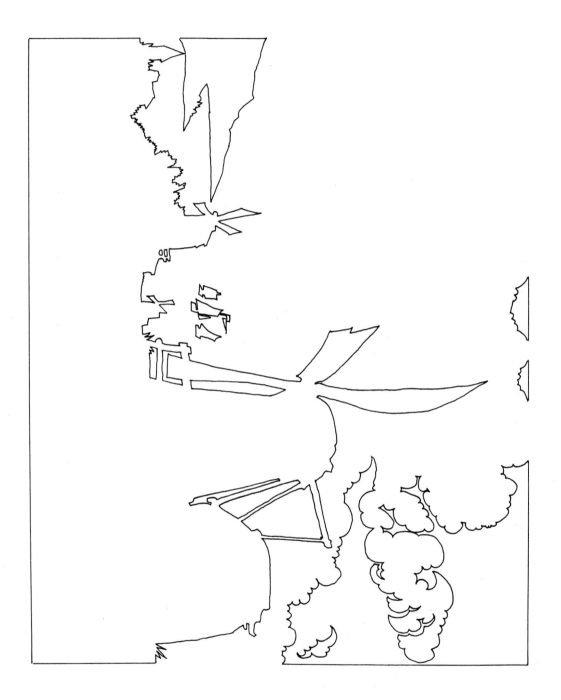

Locomotive #1

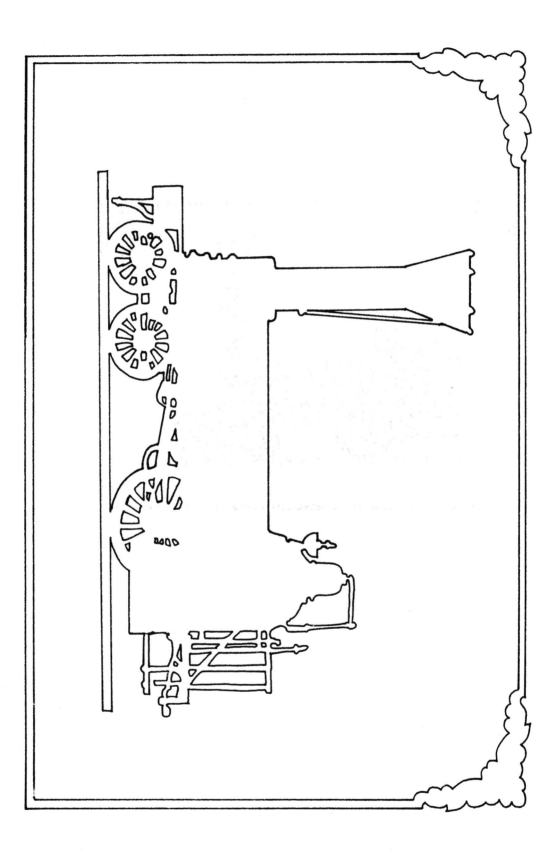

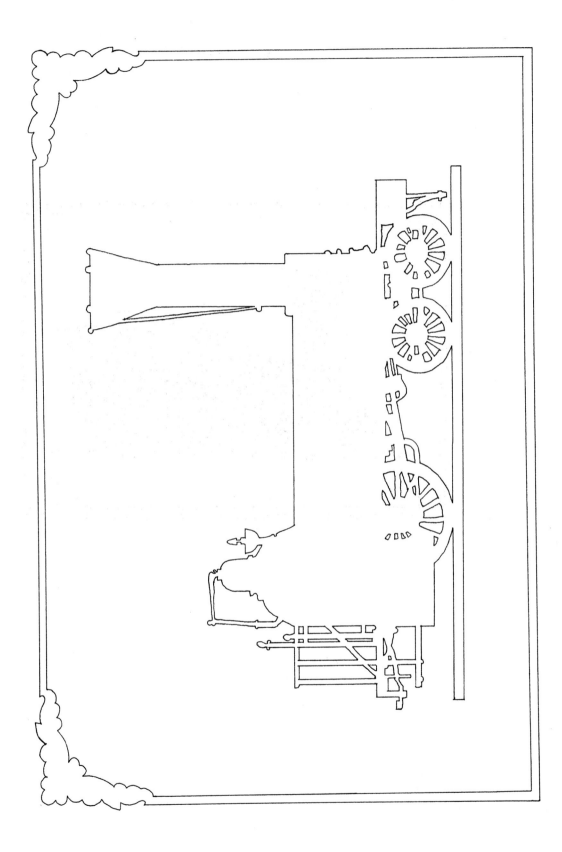

Locomotive #2

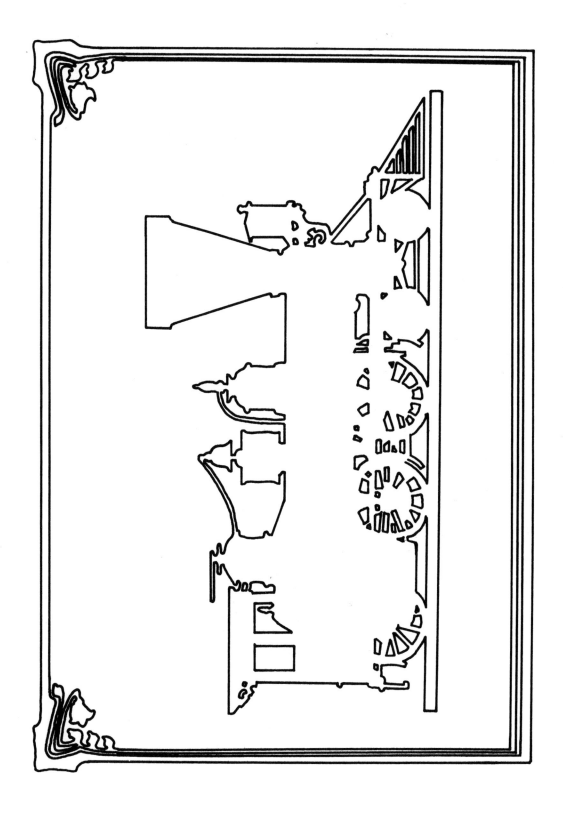

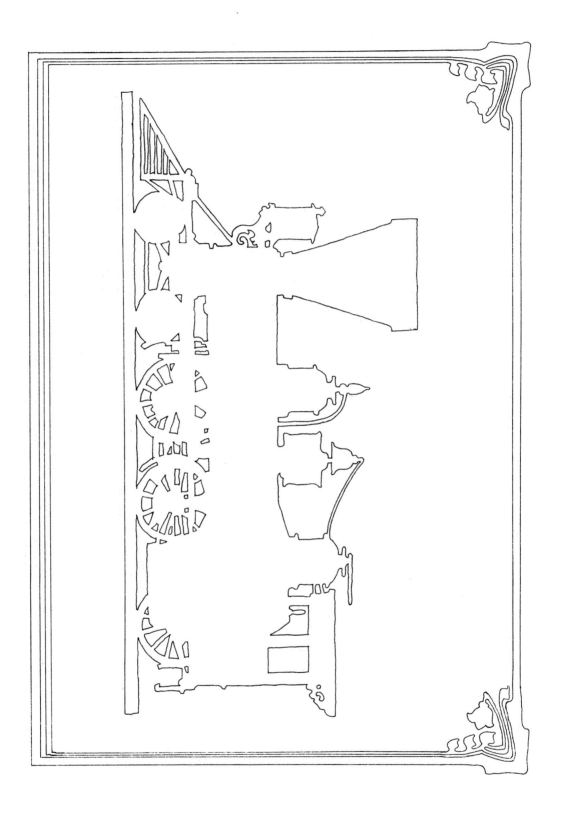

Ship #1

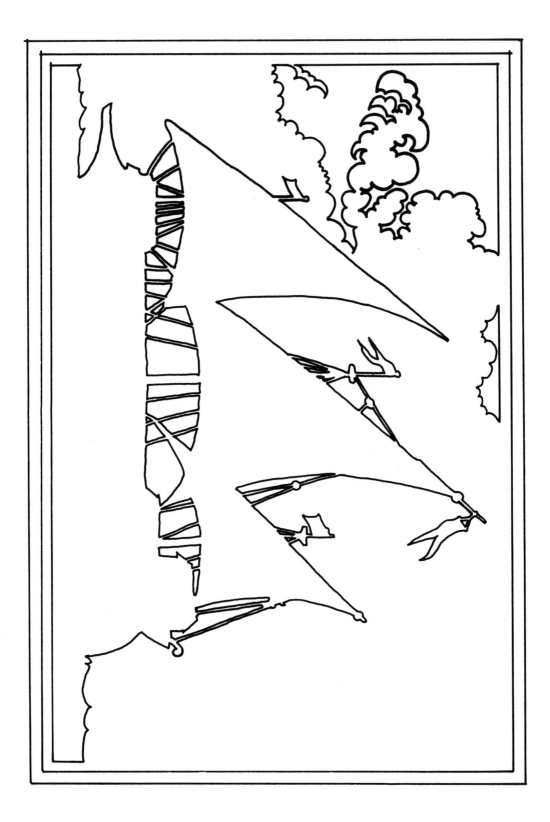

Ship #2

Model T

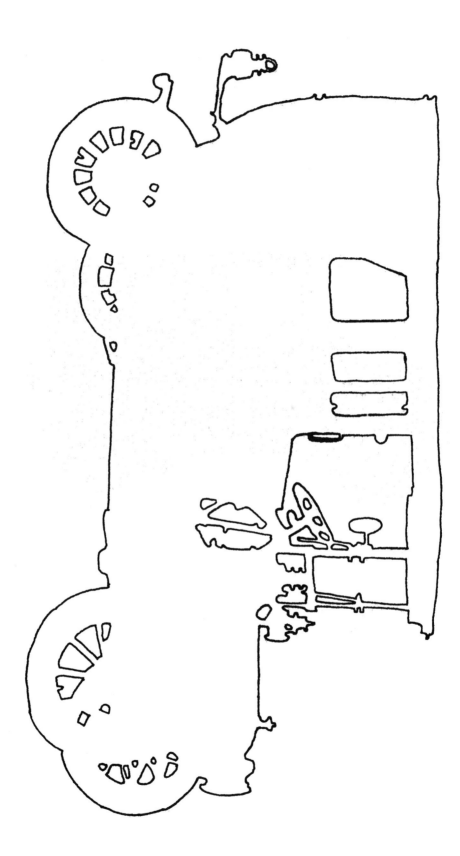

7

Framing

The frame for a silhouette is as important to the silhouettist as the planting dish is to a bonsai gardener. The frame is part of the total effect and so should not be a tacked-on afterthought. The shape, color, and character of the frame must be considered when you get ready to assemble the silhouette. A mat is sometimes used in framing silhouettes. The mat is a border around the picture and is usually of a subtle color, which complements the white board the silhouette is mounted on.

You can buy commercial prefab frame kits and assemble the pieces, make your own frame, or have the silhouette framed professionally. The frame you make yourself is, of course, the most inexpensive.

Design

A frame should blend with the style of the work being presented and be in proportion to the silhouette; it must never overpower or understate it. Because it is black, a silhouette is dramatic, and so can take a somewhat ornate frame as well as a simple wood or metal molding. The shape of the frame may be oblong, hexagonal, round, or oval; an oval frame is most appropriate for a profile silhouette.

The frame should be black, silver, or gold; bright colors tend to drown the black silhouette.

Mats

A mat or an insert provides a transition between the silhouette and the frame. Mats can be textured or smooth, in a pastel or bright color. For silhouettes, use a black, beige, or neutral-colored mat. Grass cloth, silk, and linen are good materials for the mats. (Velvet was frequently used in the 1800s.)

Generally a mat is about 1/2 inch wider on the bottom than on the top and sides. Pictures should be hung at eye level, so if the mat distances were the same on all sides, the picture would appear to the viewer to be falling out of the frame. The extra width at the bottom, which creates a larger border, corrects the inaccurate perception of the eye and puts the picture in the proper plane.

To cut a mat you need a steel T-square and an X-Acto knife. Cut the mat from the back, using the T-square as a guide. Draw the knife

You can buy commercial mats such as these, or you can make your own.

slowly and evenly down the mat, over and over in the same line, until the center piece falls out.

The oval mat is somewhat more difficult to cut and takes some experience, but because it is the most appropriate mat for profile silhouettes, it pays to master the cutting involved. You can also buy commercial mats that are already cut. Some are shown in the photograph. They come in oval or rectangular shapes and are available at art stores.

Basic Frame Construction

Picture moldings are sold at frame shops, and builder's moldings can be bought at lumber yards. The latter may not have rabbeted frames (a rabbet is an indentation that holds the picture), so ask about this feature. The rabbeted molding is easier to work with than the straight molding.

When measuring a frame to fit a silhouette, measure from outer edge to outer edge to get the overall size. The size of the frame depends on the silhouette being framed, of course, but you want to leave enough space between the figure or object and the inner edge of the frame. For small silhouettes (profiles, for example) a 3-inch

You can buy frames at art stores and craft shops. Select a suitable style for your silhouette.

If you want to make your own frame, buy a miter box. It makes cutting angle cuts easy.

margin plus a 3-inch mat is very suitable. However, you might want a larger expanse of white separating the silhouette from the frame, so these dimensions are not absolute. Just avoid too much margin or the picture will be out of scale.

To make frames you need a miter box. You can make one, but they are not very expensive so you may want to buy one. The miter box will help you cut accurate 45-degree angles at each end of the moldings. Measure the four molding strips, leaving some excess at each end for the miter cuts. Add on twice the width of the molding strip to each piece plus 1 inch or so as margin for error in sawing. For example, if you use a 2-inch-wide strip to frame a picture that is 17 inches wide, including the mat, you need to measure and cut a piece of molding 17 inches plus 2 times 2 inches plus 1 inch for error. Thus, 17 + 4 + 1 = 22 inches. Use the same measurements for top and bottom of frame, and follow the same procedure for side pieces.

First cut the molding at a 90-degree angle. Now set the miter box and saw for right-hand 45-degree angle cuts. Make these cuts. When you have cut one end of each of the four moldings with a right-hand 45-degree angle, recheck the lengths of the strips against the silhouette board ends and make all the left-hand 45-degree angle cuts.

Apply an all-purpose white glue to the mitered edges, making sure to use enough to form a strong bond. Let the glued corner dry; then repeat the process with the other corners. When all the corners are dry, put small nails in the corners to further ensure a sturdy frame. Drill holes in the back for eyelet screws so that you can hang the silhouette.

Backings

To keep dust out of the picture, seal the silhouette with brown kraft paper. Apply the white glue around the perimeter of the frame, dampen the kraft paper, and lay it in place. Smooth it down until it adheres to the frame. The paper should be taut when it dries. Trim off the excess paper 1/4 inch from the frame back with an X-Acto knife.

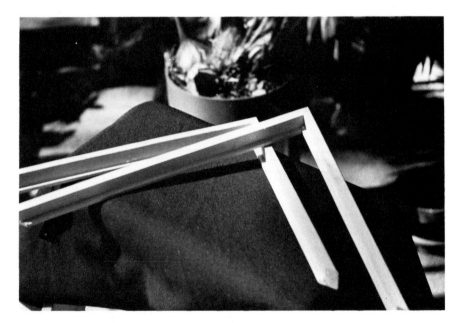

This is picture frame molding cut in a miter box; it has been glued and nailed at corners. Note the rabbet (notch) for the board.

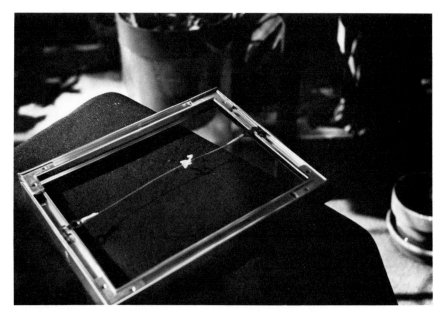

A commercial metal frame you put together yourself

Some suitable frames for silhouettes. The oval at right is especially appropriate for profiles. It has convex glass.

8

Boxes and Canisters

The application of silhouettes to boxes or canisters provides pretty decoration for little effort and cost. You can make a box yourself from pine or plywood, or use any plain box you might have at home. In salvage stores look for wooden boxes that are not too large. Any box you use should be sanded thoroughly, cleaned, and smoothed; pine or some other light wood will show off the silhouette to its full advantage. Commercial boxes will be sanded and ready for silhouettes.

You can also use wooden plaques for silhouettes and hang them like pictures. Buy an oval wooden cutting board, or just buy a piece of raw lumber and sand and smooth it for silhouette application.

Canisters are another good subject for silhouettes; some decoration can make them quite handsome. Applied in repeats, silhouettes can be a pleasing pattern on a canister or box.

The main idea with any object you choose to decorate with silhouettes is to make a pleasing design. Plan and then create a total design on the object; let each individual cutout work with the others. The effect should be a continuous flow of pattern, not spotty or slapped-on.

Lay down the cut-out pieces and arrange and rearrange them until you strike a pleasing design. There should be balance and proportion; that is, the pieces should be neither too large nor too small, but should have a pleasing overall relationship. Once you have a general idea about the design, stand back and take another look. Things always look different from a distance, and in most cases boxes and such will not be viewed close up.

For the most part, the objects we are working with are small — never more than 12 by 16 inches — so you do not want too much pattern. There should be just enough to create a happy relationship between the black silhouette and the object's surface.

Leaves and flowers are especially suitable for boxes and canisters. Do not be afraid to intertwine and overlay the silhouettes. (For information about gluing and finishing objects, see the end section of this chapter.)

Sanding

Once you have the box or plaque you want, you can use it as it is or paint it. If you want to paint it, sand the wood to get a smooth surface and remove surface blemishes. Use medium-heavy sandpaper and take your time: you want the box surface to be as smooth as glass. When your item is smooth, paint it. White is the best background for silhouettes, although beige and ochre can be quite handsome. Use glossy finish or matte finish enamel; silhouettes will look fine on either. After the paint dries, go over the box or plaque with a light-weight sandpaper, again aiming for a glass-smooth finish. Wipe and clean the wood thoroughly, and apply the final coat of

For silhouette work on boxes and canisters, you need adhesive, clear varnish, a brush, sandpaper, and cut pattern.

Trace pattern as previously described and cut out silhouette pieces. Before cementing, place pattern so that you can determine where each piece looks best.

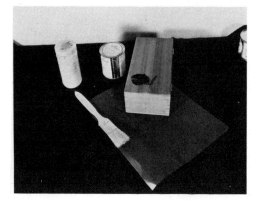

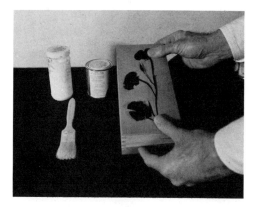

enamel. When the enamel is dry, the box will be ready for silhouette patterns. Look for a pattern in Chapter 6 or make your own.

Gluing

Gluing silhouettes on boards is quite simple, but gluing on boxes or canisters takes more time and care. First place the pieces of the silhouette on the box as you want them to appear in the final arrangement. Then take off each piece, one at a time, and squirt a drop or so of glue on the back of the silhouette cutout. Spread the glue over the surface with your finger so that the surface is fully covered and the glue is not so thick that it will ooze out when the silhouette is applied to the wood.

Do gluing on a desk, table, kitchen countertop, or, ideally, a pane of glass. Glass costs money, but it is the best surface to glue on; other surfaces may stick to the design when you try to lift it. All edges of the cutout must be securely glued in place.

Varnishing

When the silhouette design is glued and dried, preserve the entire surface by varnishing it. Varnishes form protective coatings on wood. You can use a superclear high gloss finish or a satin sheen finish. I have also used Varethane varnish and polyurethane varnish; polyurethane was the best.

Apply paste to underside of silhouette paper; use a thin layer.

After pattern is cemented to box, apply a clear varnish overcoat.

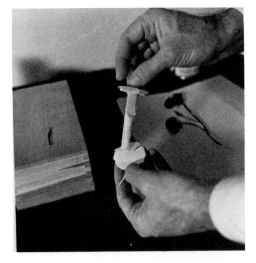

Use a good clean brush for varnishing, and sort of float the varnish on: brush it on in even and thick broad strokes in one direction, and then lightly brush in the other direction, using just the tip of the brush. Then put the box or canister aside and let it dry overnight.

When the varnish is dry (not tacky), sand the box or cannister with black superfine sandpaper. If you used a fairly thick silhouette paper like Chrome Glow, you will need two or three coats of varnish before sanding. After sanding, varnish again; you can repeat the process as many times as you want, depending on your patience. The idea is to achieve enough buildup to cover the silhouette so it cannot be pulled up.

Briefly, you should keep in mind these varnishing rules:
1. Use thin coats of varnish rather than thick ones.
2. Be sure each coat is bone dry before you apply the next one.
3. When you sand the varnished surface, *do it with a very light hand;* you do not want to scratch through to the silhouette.
4. Wet the sandpaper lightly before sanding.

After varnish dries, apply another coat and let dry. Then lightly sandpaper silhouette. Apply varnish again. This process can be repeated several times, until a completely smooth shiny surface is achieved.

9

Silhouette Sculpture

If you ever folded a paper airplane when you were a child, you did some rudimentary paper sculpture. Making small sculptures — mobiles, place cards, ornaments — out of paper is easy and fast and offers much pleasure for little effort. The secret to silhouette sculpture is the basic folding techniques that create the shapes, but these are easily mastered after a few attempts.

Try a simple experiment in paper sculpture: take a piece of silhouette paper (or any paper) and make four even folds in it; now stand the paper up on edge. You have achieved a three-dimensional shape like a piece of sculpture. By folding, cutting, and pasting one piece of paper you can create an almost infinite number of shapes. Let yourself be governed only by your imagination.

Folding

Folding and cutting paper will produce many different shapes that can be used in a variety of designs. Using straight edges with slanted and flat planes can give you ornaments that stand by themselves; place cards, figures, and so forth. Rolling and curving the silhouette paper can also create shapes that can be used in conjunction with straight and flat planes. You can make geometric folds, cones, and a variety of curved and rolled shapes from your silhouette paper.

Combine separate shapes, run a little glue down the edges of the shapes that need fixing, and glue them to bigger ones. For a support, use cardboard, pasteboard, or chipboard. Cut the support to the shape. Lightly glue the underside of each of the silhouette paper shapes and transfer it to the support, allowing it to dry before gluing in place the next shape.

To fold, turn paper over along the line you want to fold. Press along this line by sharpening the crease with your fingertips or the back of a dull knife. If you think this will leave a mark on the silhouette paper, put a piece of clean scrap paper over the area before pressing the crease. Press gently to avoid cutting into the paper. If you want a curved crease, bend the paper up or down to get the desired effect. Here are some basic folds and creases.

Zig-Zag Fold

Lay the paper flat. Fold a strip upward from the near edge so that the sides are aligned and press the strip to a sharp crease. Turn the paper over and fold the strip again, up the new side. Keep doing this, turning the sheet before making each new fold, until you reach the top. This creates a zig-zag fold.

Geometric Fold

Lay a sheet of paper flat. Fold a strip upward from the near edge at right angles to one side, and press it into a crease. Fold the strip again up on the same side of the sheet, and then turn over the paper and fold twice up the new side. Keep doing this, turning the sheet every two folds.

Roll-Over Fold

Lay a sheet of paper flat. Start at the nearest edge to you and fold a strip upward at right angles to the sides. Press the strip into a sharp crease. Fold the strip again up the same side of the sheet and continue doing so until you reach the top. Then unfold the paper like a scroll.

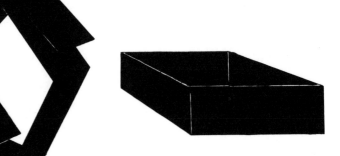

ROLL·OVER CUT

GEOMETRIC

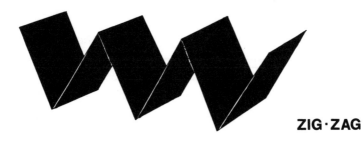

ZIG·ZAG

PAPER SCULPTURES

Fan Fold

Cut out a circle of paper and put a mark in the center. Make light marks at even intervals around the circumference; each space will be the width of a half-fold. Cut straight from one of these marks to the center. Put the paper flat and turn up the cut edge to meet the next mark and press sharply from the center, making the half-fold. Turn the circle over and fold here by lining up the first half exactly with the edge underneath. Fold. Turn the circle over and turn up the fold to meet the next mark. Press out from the center, making half of the second fold. Turn the circle over and complete the fold. Continue until all folds are made. Open the fan.

Star-Shaped Fold

Cut out a square of paper and lay it flat. Fold the paper in half lengthwise and crease it. Now open it. Crease the paper in half the other way and open it. Turn the square over. Fold it in half, corner to corner, the other way, and open the paper. Press in the paper gently from the sides to form the star.

Pyramid Fold

Draw a square for the base, and on one side of the square draw an isosceles triangle. Draw a circle, using the apex of the triangle as the circle's center and one of the sides as its radius. Where the baseline cuts the circle, mark off the length of the base three times more around the circle. Join mark to mark with straight lines and each mark to the center. You should have four joined triangles with a common apex. Draw flaps and cut out the shape. Score along dotted lines and form the pyramid. Glue the base flaps to the inside bottom edges of the pyramid, and glue the side flap inside to close the pyramid.

Cone

Draw and cut out a circle of paper. Make a straight cut from the circumference to the center. Pass one straight edge over the other to make the cone. Allow for only a narrow overlap, and then mark the inside layer at the bottom edge of the cone. Cut from the mark to the center and trim away surplus. Run a dab of glue over the overlap and hold edges together so the glue sets.

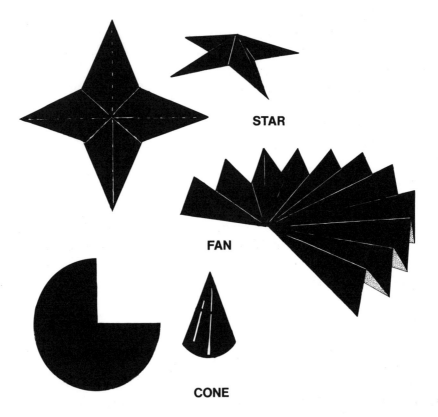

STAR

FAN

CONE

...more paper sculptures

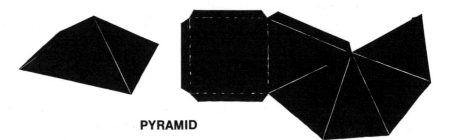

PYRAMID

The basic shapes you have made can be used in a variety of ways — interlocking, adjoining, and so forth — to create many items. Some shapes can be mounted on boards; others can be freestanding; some can be used as mobiles or — the star, for example — as hanging ornaments. Once you master the basic folding steps, there are many ways to use the paper silhouette sculptures.

Making Sculptures

There is an enormous number of paper sculptures you can make on your own. Here we offer an alligator, a butterfly, lion, and flower; these can be used as party favors, as place cards, and so on. The basic processes of making any paper sculpture, whether they are ornaments, mobiles, or what-have-you, remain the same.

On a folded piece of silhouette paper trace alligator pattern.

Cut out alligator with scissors.

Cut notches as shown.

Completed alligator

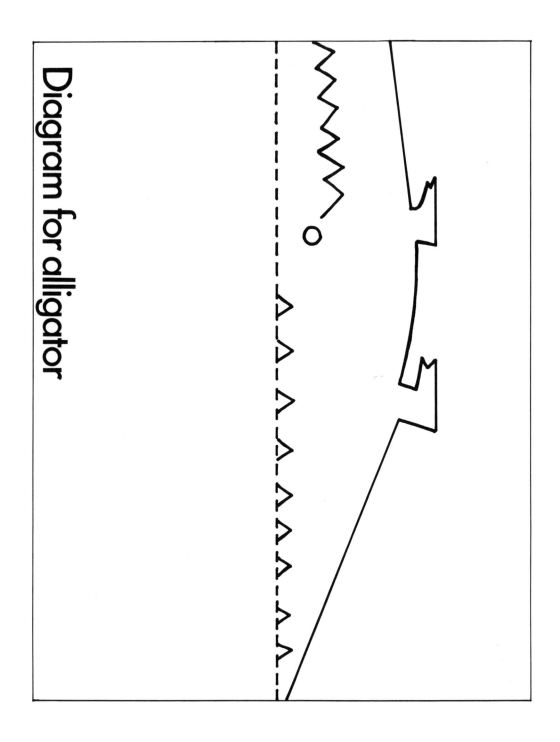

Diagram for alligator

To make an alligator

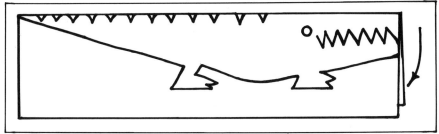

1. Start with rectangular paper. Trace diagram, and fold in half.

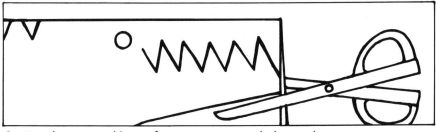

2. Cut along traced lines; for eyes, use paper hole puncher.

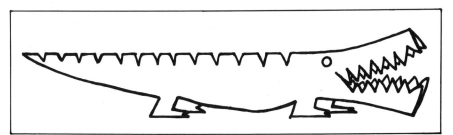

3. Lift top jaw by holding bottom jaw firmly. Cut grooves on back of alligator. Separate legs so that cut out can stand on all four legs.

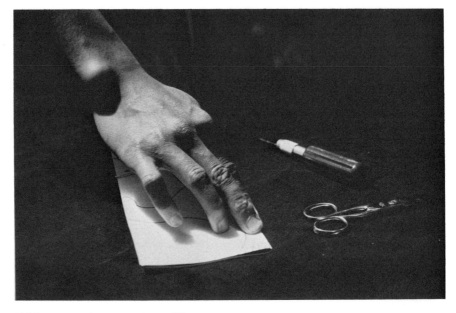

Fold paper and trace pattern of lion.

Cut out lion.

Fold as shown.

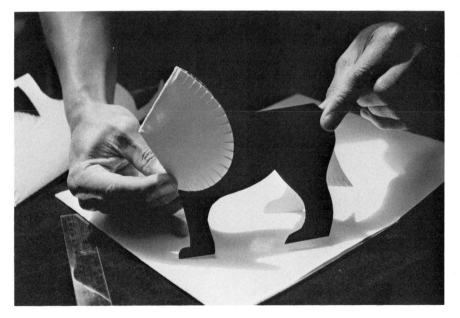

Completed lion

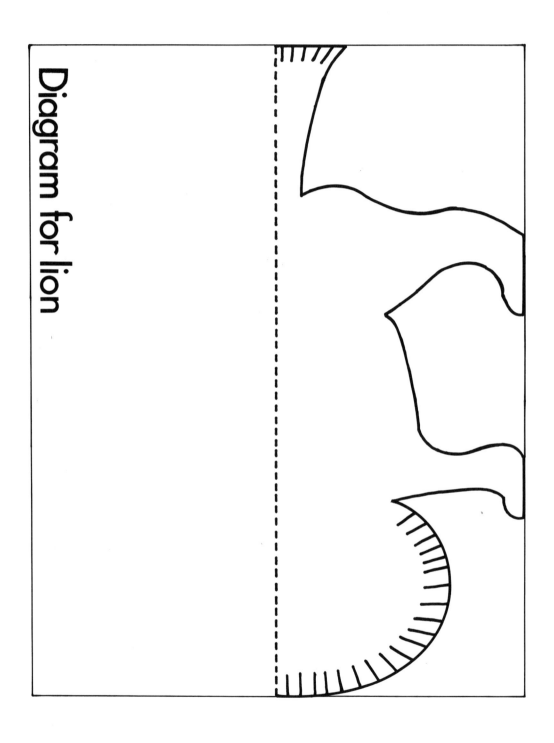

Diagram for lion

To make a lion

1. Start with rectangular paper and trace diagram using carbon paper underneath. Fold along dotted line.

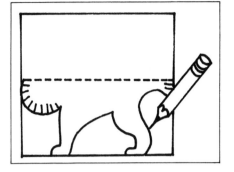

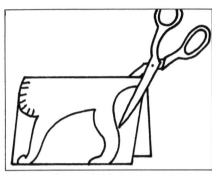

2. Cut along solid lines.

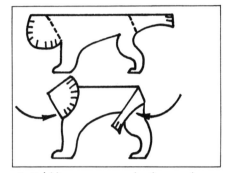

3. Fold lion's mane and tail toward you as shown.

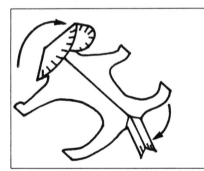

4. Open work and push mane back. Push tail down; crease.

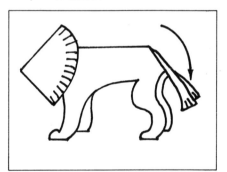

5. Completed lion should stand on its own.

Trace pattern of flower.

Cut out as shown.

Roll corners if desired.

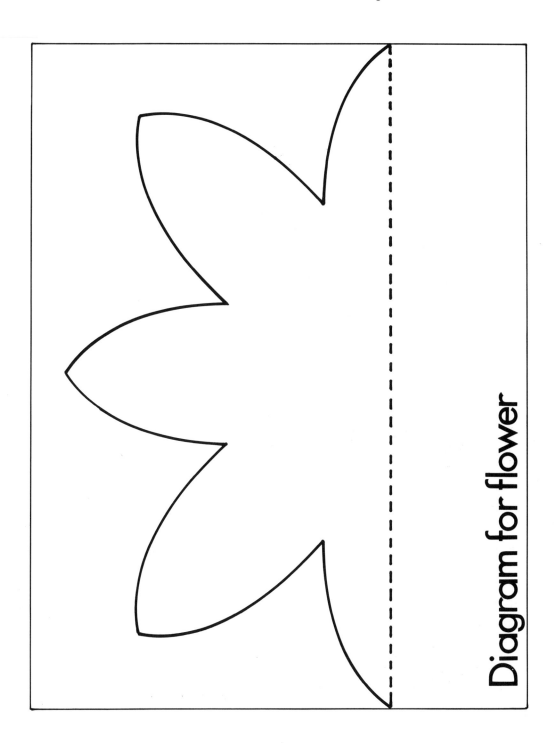

Diagram for flower

To make a flower

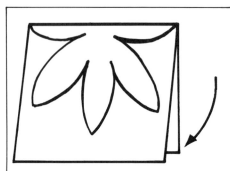

1. Use square paper. Trace diagram, then fold down as shown.

2. MIDDLE-LEFT Cut pattern.

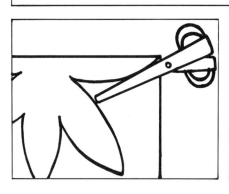 

3. ABOVE Open flower and curl ends with pencil.

4. Finished flower

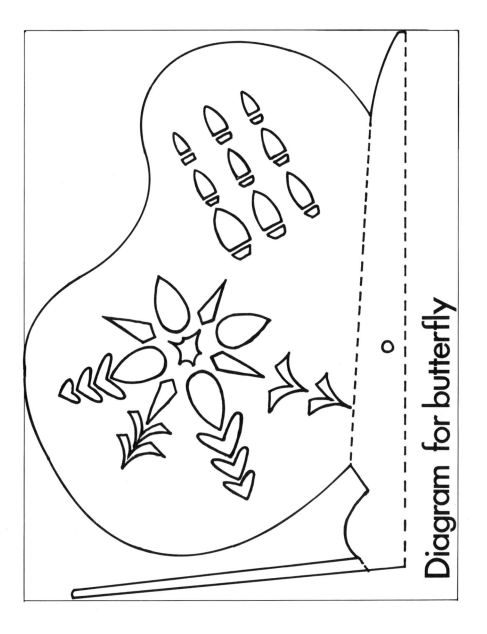

Diagram for butterfly

To make a butterfly

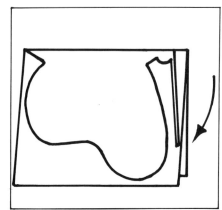

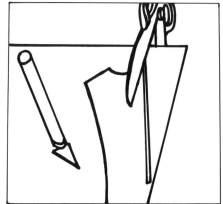

1. Start with large square, trace outline diagram, and fold.

2. Cut outline with scissors. Use sharp knife for small area.

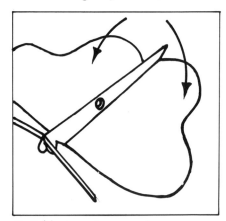

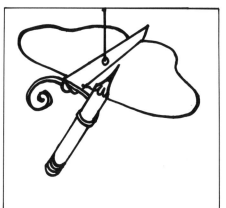

3. Fold wings down as shown; with paper hole puncher, make hole in body.

4. Insert and tie string in hole to suspend butterfly. Curl antennae with pencil.

10

Appliqué Silhouettes

Appliqué stitchery is the sewing of one fabric onto another fabric. It is somewhat like collage, in which objects or pieces of paper in various shapes are pasted on a surface to form an artistic whole. The appliqué decoration is particularly handsome and dramatic when done in silhouette. The pattern of black fabric against a pastel background creates a striking effect. The appliqué can be used to decorate pillows, quilts, tote bags, place mats, or other such items.

Patterns

Practically any pleasing pattern can be used for silhouette appliqué but nature provides many favorite subjects: flowers, insects, butterflies, fruit. Simple patterns are more in keeping with this kind of sewing, and complicated designs should be avoided. As with the paper silhouette, it is the outline against the background that is important.

The appliquéd lines may be graceful and curved, geometric or straight-edged. It is best to start with a pattern based on only a few shapes; later you can try designs involving more shapes.

The running stitch and the blind stitch are the most popular stitches for applying the silhouette appliqué and are the easiest to master.

Making the Pattern

Select a pattern that is appropriate to the piece being appliquéd. You can use a pattern from this book or find a picture in a magazine or a newspaper ad from which to make a pattern. Here are the basic steps to follow in pattern-making:

1. Make a tracing of the pattern on a piece of paper. (Use carbon paper.)
2. Place the paper pattern on Dritz tracing paper over the fabric that you are using for the background. (Dritz tracing paper may be bought at fabric shops.) Outline the pattern with the wheel cutter (also available at fabric stores).
3. Pencil a second pattern from the original tracing on cardboard; cut out the pieces.
4. With a soap marker outline the cardboard pieces on the black material, which will be used for appliquéing.
5. Cut out the black pieces.
6. Place the black pieces so they match the first pattern.
7. Sew the appliqué in place.

Materials for appliqué silhouette work

Trace pattern on paper.

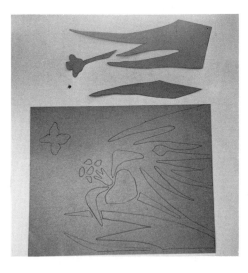

Above left:
Put pattern over Dritz carbon; Dritz paper over pillow material.

Above right:
Pattern on pillow material

Middle left:
Trace pattern on cardboard. Cut out pieces.

Middle right:
Trace outline of cardboard pieces on black felt.

Left:
Cut felt pieces, which you will place over pattern drawn on pillow.

Finished pillow

Black silhouettes make a stunning place mat. Not very practical, though.

How you place the pattern and arrangement of the cutouts is what makes the design. As in most designs, there should be proportion and balance, and each object should relate to the other. Arrangements, particularly of flowers, stems, and leaves, should not be too formal. There is great latitude in appliqué, and what you ultimately do depends on just how proficient you are at it. You might be a superb appliqué worker, but you will never know until you start.

Basic Appliqué Stitches

The two most simple stitches for appliquéing are the running stitch and the blind stitch. The running stitch keeps the fabric flat and adds a small-scale stitch pattern at the edges. The blind stitch (or hemming stitch) is concealed and makes the fabric stand away from the background.

For the running stitch, knot a single strand of thread. Then draw the needle through the back of both layers of fabric and sew. Consistency of stitch length comes through practice. Keep the edges of the appliqué firmly tucked under and the stitches very near the edge. Keep the cut shape toward you so that you sew on the outer edge. Let your left thumb hold the appliqué in place (or your right thumb if you are left-handed). When you come to corners, fold under only one edge to start. Then turn under the second edge. Do not try to fold under both edges of the corner at the same time. On an inside corner the fabric must be clipped. Then stitch down one edge and do not fold under the second until you have reached the corner.

For the blind stitch, use thread the same color as the fabric. Knot a single thread at the end. Turn under the edge of the fabric to be appliquéd, and draw the thread through from behind so that it emerges on the fold. As you stitch, the thread will be hidden either behind the backing fabric or within the fold of the piece you are appliquéing. Corners are sewed much the same way as with the running-stitch method. One edge is blind-stitched until the folded-under hem is reached. Then the piece is turned and the sewing continued on the next side, with the hem folded under.

Another stitch you may want to use is the whip stitch, which is good for reinforcing and closing seams. Bring the thread through from behind. Then move the needle above the appliqué material. This way the thread binds the edge.

Embroidery stitches can decorate the appliqué itself or be added as accent areas here and there, depending on the design or pattern you are creating.

What to Appliqué

Appliqués in silhouette are effective on quilts, coverlets, tote bags, pillows; they may even be used as pictures for hanging in a room. Let us look at some easy items to appliqué for beginning projects.

Pillows

A pillow is small enough to finish in a short time and yet versatile enough to allow you to apply almost any type of silhouette pattern. A simple pattern is the most effective one for a pillow because you do not want too much embellishment; you want just enough to add some distinction to the piece.

Quilts

A quilt is a good object for silhouettes in simple patterns of repeated blocks or circles in patchwork style. There is no intricate cutting or detailing to be done on the silhouette, and stitching is relatively easy. Good repeat patterns are small deer for a child's quilt or simple geometric blocks for a standard quilt.

Tote Bags

Tote bags are another good beginning project. They can be used as school bags, picnic bags, or carryalls. Like the pillow, the tote bag is small enough for floral patterns, insect shapes, or simple stars — not elaborate, yet handsome in their simplicity.

Wall Hangings

These are interesting projects to do after you have made one or two other items. You can let your imagination go and create striking patterns of many kinds. Since the wall hanging will always be on display, it takes more thought and planning than, say, a tote bag. The fabric for the wall hanging should be backed, hemmed, and finished before the appliqué is stitched on. Only then should you start the pattern work and sewing of the appliqué.

Place Mats

The plain place mat has its uses but the decorated one is always more handsome. Silhouette work lends itself well to place mats, and simple floral designs are always pleasing.

11

Shade or Shadow Pictures

The term *shade or shadow picture* technically refers to a silhouette either cut from paper or painted on the back of a piece of convex glass and framed in such a way that it is held at least 1 inch from a white canvas board background. Thus, the beauty of the piece is in the shadow or shade reflected on the background from changing light.

The shadow or shade is difficult to execute and requires precise framing to work properly. I suggest you attempt it only after you have done some standard paper silhouettes. The materials are not expensive, but some skill is necessary to achieve the ultimate result.

Materials Needed

You will need all the materials mentioned in Chapter 2, in addition to a white board (preferably oval) and a piece of glass. Convex glass (bowed out on one surface, like a hubcap) can be bought at glass stores, but it is expensive and hard to find. A much easier way of getting everything you need including convex glass is to buy a

A silhouette held 1 inch from a white board creates a shadow picture.

ready-made frame that has this bowed glass in it; art stores and some Woolworth branches carry these frames. The frames come in three sizes — 5, 7, and 9-inch ovals — and are 1 inch wide. The glass is 1 inch from the easel back, which makes these ideal mounts for the shade picture.

How to Do It

I have found that the best way to make the shadow picture is to paint the silhouette on the *reverse* side of the glass (the hollow side). Profiles of people or animals are the most effective; anything compli-

A commercial frame shown here is ideal for shade pictures. The frame comes with convex glass, 1-inch metal frame, insert holder (center), white paper, and easel back.

cated does not adapt to shade work because too much negative area, or cutouts with too many details, defeats the purpose. A simple profile in black without any detailing at all works best. Make the pattern with a grease pencil on the glass, and then, as explained in Chapter 5, paint the profile with even brush strokes or a hatching effect. You want this profile to be as precise as possible so that the shadow reflected on the background board is clearly defined.

Another way of making a shadow is to use the paper method. Cut out the silhouette and apply it to the back of the glass (remember that, whether painted or cut from paper, the image will always be reversed when you turn over the glass). When you have cut the silhouette, lay it in place on the glass. Now take a sheet of flexible clear thin plastic, such as Saran Wrap, cut it to the size of the frame, and put a few dabs of paste on the glass area around the silhouette. Press the plastic against the silhouette, and tuck the edges into the outer band of the frame to secure the silhouette in place. (The little dabs of paste will help too.) Then mount the white backing and secure the easel back in place.

Applying the clear plastic sheet is difficult, so practice a few times before you attempt the final cut.

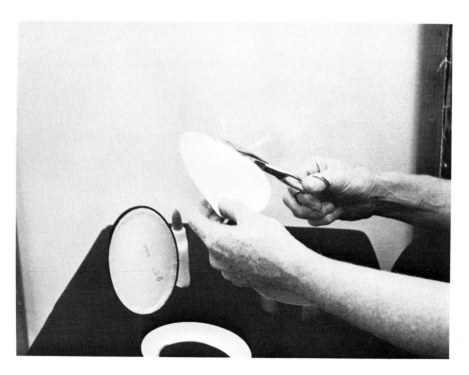

Cut out glassine oval to size of paper back.

Insert silhouette, white side up, and cover with glassine. Add dabs of glue at edges between glass and glassine sheet.

Press glassine against glass for a few seconds. Smooth out. The silhouette will stay centered.

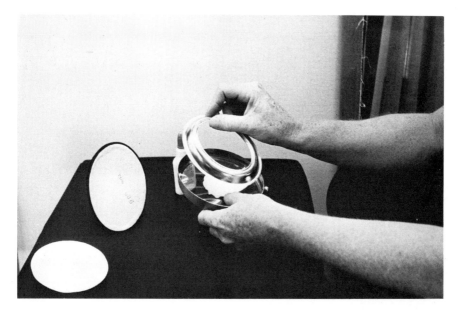

Insert the metal liner that comes with the frame to further secure the glassine against silhouette.

Place white backing against the easel and attach the easel with the pins which come with the frame.

In this particular picture, which was taken outdoors, the sun's reflection diminishes the shadow somewhat. In a picture taken indoors, the shadow would be more defined.

12

Variations

Throughout this book we have given you patterns, suggestions, and ideas for various types of silhouettes. This closing chapter covers some variations on silhouette art.

Flowers

Portrait flowers always make handsome silhouettes because of their graceful lines and shapes. If you have ever pressed flowers in a book, you know what I mean. In doing flower work, try to capture the details of the inside of the flower; they will enhance the silhouette. It is the combination of hollow-cut and solid-cut work that will achieve the desired effect. Remember to cut out the flower from one piece of paper; do not get fancy and try to make several patterns and paste them together in a composite form. It will not work — it will look exactly like a put-together piece. Work carefully and delicately on flower portraits. With some experience and patience, you can make these pictures works of art, suitable for your silhouette library.

Select pictures of flowers from a magazine or a book. Outline them on tracing paper and then transfer them to the silhouette paper. If you are adept at sketching, you can draw your own flowers and cut them out.

Leaves

The outlines of leaves are varied; they are deeply lobed or scalloped or ragged or toothed. Veining in leaves also differs. For example, some leaves have parallel veins, whereas others have networks of veins. Cutting leaf silhouettes is excellent practice, and leaf pictures can be very handsome. A black leaf with white veining would be a solid cut; a white leaf with black veining would be a hollow cut. For practice it is fine to cut single leaves, but for a complete picture you will want several leaves in one frame. This kind of silhouette can be used in a glass-bottomed serving tray or can be hung as wall plaques.

Butterflies and Insects

These wonderful forms offer a multitude of silhouette pleasures. Butterflies are especially appropriate for silhouettes. You cannot get insects or butterflies to pose for you, so trace them from magazine pictures with tissue paper and then transfer the pattern to silhouette paper. For butterflies, trace only one wing and then use two pieces of silhouette paper when cutting; you thus get the other wing for free.

Nature Scenes

If you choose to draw a scene from nature you may, perhaps, find it the most difficult to execute. Since you are not tracing from a pattern, you must sketch freehand, and the scene must be stylized into more or less block forms to conform to silhouette work. It is best to make several sketches of the same scene. Refine the best sketch and make a pattern from it.

With nature scenes, concentrate only on a small portion of the setting. Do not attempt a broad canvas; it just does not transfer well to a silhouette. Do small pictures but do them well.

Embellishing the Silhouette

Some amount of appropriate detailing can be done with paint on silhouettes, such as hair or collars, but too much painting will ruin the ordinary silhouette. You want to stroke in details ever so carefully. The best pigments to use are silver or gold or, for dramatic contrast, Chinese white. Use a sable brush with a fine point (double 0 is satisfactory).

The painting of details on a silhouette can be done either after it is mounted on a board or before you mount it. In any case, be sure the paint is thoroughly dry so that it will not smear if you touch it in the process of framing.